A Celtic Eucharist

A Celtic Eucharist

Compiled and edited
by Brendan O'Malley

MOREHOUSE PUBLISHING

Copyright © 2002 Brendan O'Malley

Morehouse Publishing
P.O. Box 1321
Harrisburg, PA 17105

*Morehouse Publishing is a division
of The Morehouse Group.*

All rights reserved. No part of this book may be reproduced or transmitted in any form or by any means, electronic or mechanical, including photocopying, recording, or by any information storage and retrieval system, without written permission from the publisher.

First published in Great Britain in 2001 by The Canterbury Press Norwich (a publishing imprint of Hymns Ancient & Modern Limited, a registered charity), St. Mary's Works, St. Mary's Plain, Norwich, Norfolk, NR3 3BH

Library of Congress
Cataloging-in-Publication Data

A Celtic Eucharist / compiled and edited by Brendan O'Malley.
    p. cm.
ISBN 0-8192-1896-0
    1. Catholic Church—Celtic rite—Liturgy—Texts. 2. Lord's Supper (Liturgy)—Texts. I. O'Malley, Brendan (Brian Brendan)
BX1995.C4 C45 2002
264'.023—dc21   2001044022

ISBN 0-8192-1896-0

Printed in the United States of America
01 02 03 04 05 06 07 08 09   9 8 7 6 5 4 3 2 1

To Stephen, Julian, John and the 'Little Ones' –
Jody and Emma
of the University of Wales, Lampeter

Before, behind, beneath,
Creation, conception, birth,
Redemption
This prayer, this moment:
Creator's Spirit.

Holy Spirit,
Infinitude
Eternally pouring forth,
Energy of love
Sustaining the universe.

Come
Creator Spirit
Conceiving Spirit
Initiating Spirit
Life-giving
Birth-giving
Spirit
Life-breath of love.

Holy Spirit
Your blessed unction from above
Is fire of love.

adapted from 'Veni Creator Spiritus'
(A Welsh Pilgrim's Manual,
Brendan O'Malley)

With the saints
>	I risked approaching
God's altar, bearing
>	my burden.
It is a table to feed the
>	starving poor.
It is a table to strengthen
>	the weak.
There I could, as it were,
>	touch
The broken body of holy
>	Jesus.
Suddenly my heart melted
Like wax before
>	the flame.

>	NICANDER

*(Revd Morris Williams;
nineteenth century)*

CONTENTS

Introduction	xiii
Suggestions for using this book	xv
A Celtic Eucharist	1
Notes	42
Appendix: Alternative prayers and sentences	43

INTRODUCTION

The question could be asked whether a 'Celtic Eucharist' consisting of ancient texts is of any use or relevance in today's world. I would answer that it is not my intention to 'mimic' an ancient Eucharist, but to link our cultural experience into the living tradition of the Church. Liturgy exists in the here and now. The Liturgy is the sacred work of the people of God, and it is a tool to carve the Kingdom of God from the raw material of creation. Its real significance is to make all things whole, to bring all things into Oneness in heaven and on earth through the symbols of the elements.

The Eucharist may be celebrated at twelve noon today, but that same liturgy has to link us back in time, even joining in the echo of worship which existed before history began. It may be seen as a pageant, or simple memorial of the First Liturgy, but it is more than that; it must bring the Apostolic City into the now, and then onwards joining with the Heavenly City. The dialogue with the past locates our present in the mainstream of Tradition, and is the guarantee of the Presence now. My 'now' exists because of tradition and within the Tradition.

In Scotland, as a child, I heard from my Grandmother about the holiness of the Eucharist, and I learned even more from her body language when present at its celebration. Now I know for myself what the Eucharist is. I am with Christ in Lampeter, Wales, when celebrating the Eucharist in the now, not with the Apostles or literally 'then' in the past, but when I look back I know that I am part of the Apostolic Tradition. As I look forward to the Eschaton my concern with the present is taken into the future. I am a part of the constant, ongoing celebration of the eternal liturgy in heaven and on earth.

A liturgy is good because it is effective. The question is, does it reflect the Tradition and does it reflect the living reality of today as well as of the past? In our case, does the Celtic Eucharist reflect the Celtic Tradition? In other words, is this the way our Celtic ancestors would have worshipped, albeit in the modern idiom? I believe that it is in the essence of that self-same Tradition. This Eucharist is offered for use in modern communities. Its words, its art and its shape are designed to serve the ongoing liturgical Celtic Tradition, reflecting a people who lived and died liturgically, and it is authentic by virtue of its being both traditional and radically new.

This collected text is very much a working liturgy. In common with the *Stowe Missal*, little in it is unique. What we do know is that the Eucharist set out here is, albeit in a modern idiom, very similar to the liturgy celebrated in a Celi De community in the early ninth century. The texts compiled here are adopted from the mainstream early Irish tradition (see notes). They fit easily into the framework of modern worship and are offered as a resource to those who are searching for an authentic 'Celtic Liturgy' in praise of the Lord of the Elements, containing all the elements of our Christian roots. I have simply followed the practice of many Celtic scribes, in that I have collected together the prayers and texts which are useful for this particular Celtic Eucharist. It is by no means exhaustive.

I wish to express my grateful thanks to the Reverend Dr Thomas O'Loughlin for his sensitive translations and suggestions. I would also like to thank Stephen Grant, my faithful Chaplaincy Assistant at the University of Wales, Lampeter, for his patience and good humour when typing the manuscript.

Brendan O'Malley
Lampeter
August 2000

SUGGESTIONS FOR USING THIS BOOK

The Optional Texts

The following sections are optional and may be left out should the celebrant so wish. The whole Liturgy need not be too wordy and pause for silence in appropriate places is to be encouraged.

The Entrance Rite: the Lorica Litany may be chanted in procession. It is a prayer for divine protection and favour.

The Ceremony of Light: this is designed for use at an evening Eucharist; it may follow the Lorica or take its place.

A Celtic Hymn: this may be chanted to a typical Magnificat chant.

The Creed: Tírechán's Creed is best recited by a lone voice and may be left out if the Lorica, Ceremony of Light and a Celtic Hymn are used.

Notes for the Celebrant

This *Celtic Eucharist* is designed to be used alongside a modern lectionary, and may equally well be placed with the Roman, Irish, Scottish, Welsh or *Common Worship* lectionaries. If the celebrant wishes to use a Bible for the Old Testament, Epistle or Gospel readings, then the additional prayers in this book may be used to advantage. They are culled from various Celtic and scriptural sources for ease of use as opening sentences and prayers, prayers over the gifts, communion sentences and closing prayers.

It may also be noticed that the Litany of the Trinity after the Ministry of the Word is used as the Rite of Penance. This is in keeping with the Celtic Rite of practice; indeed the Kyrie ('Lord have mercy') in modern liturgies is a direct descendant of such a litany as that of the *Stowe Missal*.

It seems right to me that, after the heart has been opened by the hearing of the Word of God, compunction ensues and the need to ask forgiveness of God and neighbour in the sign of peace is in order before we approach the divine table.

The important thing is to use your common sense and sense of liturgical rhythm. The optional texts indicated above are there to enhance the spirit and liturgical practice of the whole work. This is a Eucharist which needs to be celebrated sensitively, gently and in a contemplative manner, with appropriate pauses for silence.

Alternative prayers and sentences are included in the Appendix.

B. O'M.

A Celtic Eucharist

THE ENTRANCE RITE

Lorica Litany

St Patrick's Breastplate or Deer's Cry[1]

(This may be chanted in procession or a hymn version may be sung by the congregation)

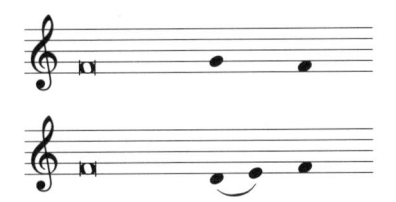

Today I shield myself with threefold pówer,
Invocation *of* the Trinity.
Belief in the threeness, profession of the óneness,
In union with *the* Creator.

Today I shield myself with the power of Christ's baptism,
his hanging and búrial,
His rising again and his ascension,
his descent for *the* last judgement.

Today I shield myself with the loving power of the Chérubim,
Obedience of angels, service *of* archangels,
Hope of rising to my reward, prayer of the pátriarchs,
Sayings of the prophets, teachings of the apostles,
faith of confessors, deeds of *righ*teous people.

Today I shield myself with the power of heaven,
Light of the sun.
Brilliance of the moon, splend*our* of fire,
Speed of lightning, swiftness of wińd,
Depths of sea, firmness of earth, hard*ness* of rock.

Today I shield myself with God's power to direćt me,
God's strength *to* uphold me,
God's good sense to gúide me,
God's ear to *listen* for me,
God's speaking to spéak for me,
God's *hand* to guard me,
God's path opening befoŕe me,
God's shield *to* protect me,
From the snares of démons,
The inducements of *my* own vices,
The proclivities of human náture,
And those who *wish* me evil.
I summon these powers to cóme
Between me and every cruel and merciless power
that threatens my body *and* my soul.

Christ be my protection todaý
***Against* violence,**
Against íllness,
***Against* drowning,**
Against mortal wóunding,
So that I may come to my ulti*ma*te reward.

Christ be wíth me,
Christ *be* before me,
Christ be behińd me,
Christ *be* inside me,
Christ be beneáth me,
Christ *be* above me,
Christ on my riǵht hand,
Christ *on* my left hand,
Christ when I lié down,
Christ *when* I sit down,
Christ when I riśe up,
Christ *all* around me.
Christ in the heart of everyone who behólds me;
Christ in every eye that sees me;
and Christ in every *ear* that hears me.

Today I shield myself with threefold power,
invocation of the Tŕinity.
Belief in the threeness, profession of the oneness,
in union with *the* Creator.

The Lord is salvátion;
Christ *is* salvation.
The Lord is salvátion;
May your salvation, O Lord, be *always* with us.

CEREMONY OF LIGHT

(for optional evening use)

Thy word is a lantern unto my feet,
and a light unto my path.

Prayer bell or gong

Celebrant: At eventide there shall be light.

(Lighting of the lamp)

Reader: Blessed are you, O Lord our God,
King of the Universe,
at your word you bring on the evening twilight.
You create day and night;
you roll away light before the darkness,
and the darkness before the light;
you make the day to pass,
and the night to approach,
and divide the day from the night.
Blessed are you, O Lord,
for you bring on the evening twilight.

Celebrant: Lighten our darkness,
we beseech you O Lord,
and of your great mercy defend us
from all perils and dangers of this night,
for the love of your only Son,
Our Saviour, Jesus Christ.
Amen.

Reader: Daylight has ended
Night is upon us
yet unto Thee
sustainer of all things
Darkness and Light,
all times and all seasons
all are as one
O Lord of Creation.

Phos Hilarion

O Gracious Light, pure brightness of the everliving | Father in | heaven.
O Jesus | Christ, | holy and blessed!
Now as we come to the | setting of the | sun,
and our eyes behold the evening | Light, we sing your praises, O | God:
Father, | Son and | Holy Spirit.
You are worthy at all times to be praised
by happy voices,*
O | Son of | God, O Giver of Life,
and to be | glorified through | all the worlds.

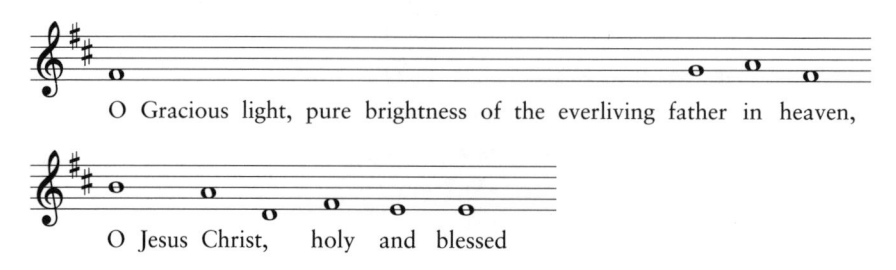

O Gracious light, pure brightness of the everliving father in heaven,

O Jesus Christ, holy and blessed

Now as we come to the setting of the sun, and our eyes behold to evening light,

We sing your praises, O God: Father, Son and Holy Spirit

You are worthy at all times to be praised by happy voices,

O Son of God, O Giver of life, and to be glorified through all the worlds.

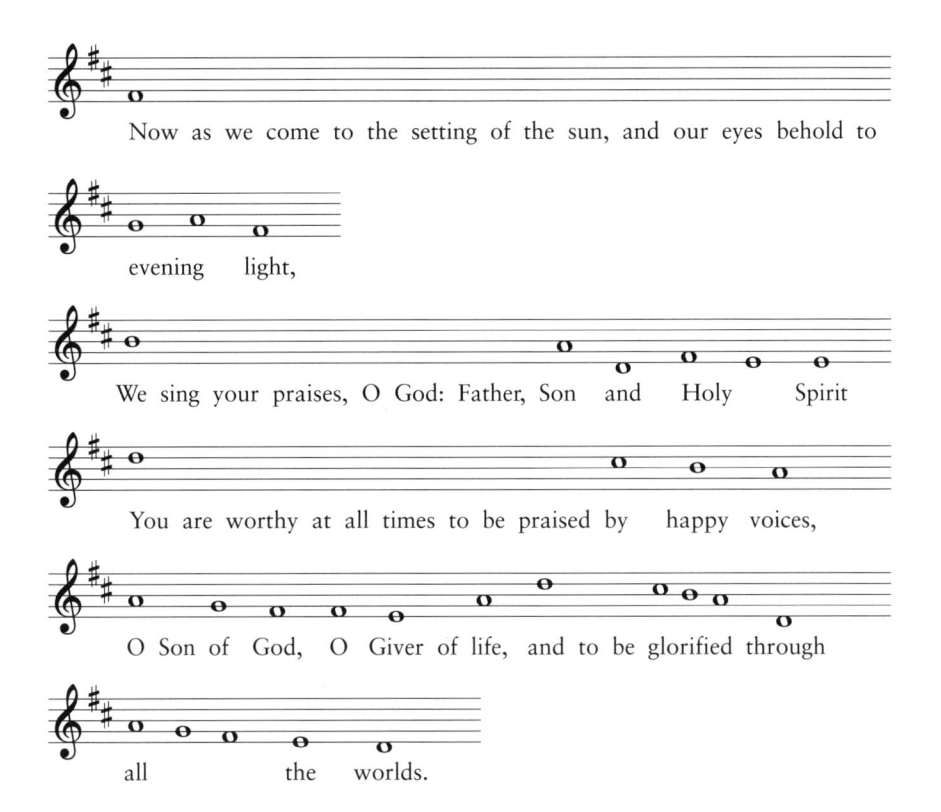

Pause

Celebrant: At this evening hour
may the understanding of all our hearts
be opened to that Light
which enlightens everyone
who comes into the world.
For this is the Light which gives us
true knowledge of the Name over all
by which God is known.

A Celtic Hymn for the Lighting of the Vesper Light[2]

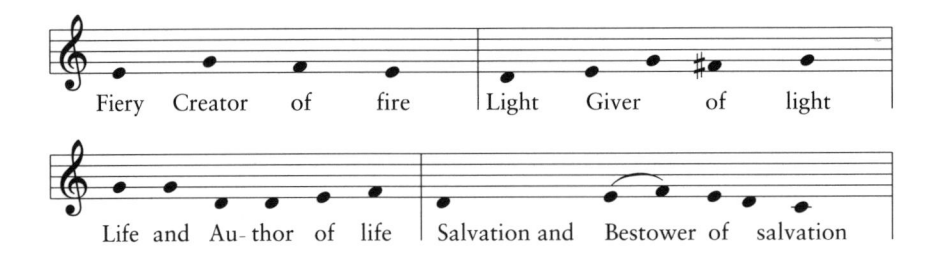

[musical notation]

Fiery Creator of fire | Light Giver of light
Life and Au-thor of life | Salvation and Bestower of salvation

I
Fiery Creator * of fire,
Light Giver | of light,
Life and Author * of life,
Salvation and | Bestower of salvation,

II
In case the lamps * should abandon
The joys | of this night,
You who do not desire * our death,
Give light to | our breast.

III
To those wandering * from Egypt,
You bestow | the double grace,
You show the veil * of cloud,
And give | the nocturnal light.

IV
With a pillar of cloud * in the day,
You protect the people | as they go,
With a pillar of fire * at evening,
You dispel the | night with light.

V
You call out to your servant * from the flame,
You do not spurn | the bush of thorns,
And though you are * consuming fire,
You do not burn | what you illumine.

VI
Now it is time that the * cloudy bee-bread
Should be consumed, all | impurity boiled away
And the waxen flesh * should shine
With the glow | of the Holy Spirit.

VII
You store now in the * recesses of the comb
The sweet food | of the divine honey,
And purify the inmost * cells of the heart,
You have | filled them with your word;

VIII
That the swarm * of the new brood,
Chosen | by your mouth and spirit,
May leave their burdens * and win heaven
On wings | now free from care.

If the Lorica has not been sung the Celebrant may begin the Eucharist here with the sentence and the following greeting:

In the name of God: Father, Son and Holy Spirit,
Amen.
Grace and peace be with you,
and also with you.

If the Lorica has been sung the Eucharist continues here.

Gloria[3]

Glory to God in the highest,
and peace to his people on earth.
Lord God, heavenly King,
Almighty God and Father,
we worship you, we give you thanks,
we praise you for your glory.

Lord Jesus Christ, only Son of the Father,
Lord God, Lamb of God,
you take away the sin of the world:
have mercy on us;
you are seated at the right hand of the Father:
receive our prayer.

For you alone are the Holy One,
you alone are the Lord,
you alone are the Most High,
Jesus Christ, with the Holy Spirit,
in the glory of God the Father.
Amen.

The Collect of the Day

Let us pray.

THE MINISTRY OF THE WORD

Old and New Testament readings shall be announced:

A reading from the . . .

They shall end with the words:

This is the Word of the Lord.
Thanks be to God.

*The Gospel alone may be proclaimed
(if the Lorica and Ceremony of Light are used)*

The Lord be with you,
and also with you.

Hear the Holy Gospel according to Saint . . .
Glory to Christ our Saviour.

This is the Gospel of the Lord.
Praise to Christ our Lord.

The Homily or Address

The Creed[4]

(*May be recited by a lone voice*)

Our God is the God of all humans,
    the God of heaven and earth,
    the God of sea and rivers,
the God of the sun and moon,
the God of all the heavenly bodies,
the God of the lofty mountains,
the God of the lowly valleys.
God is above the heavens;
and he is beneath the heavens.
Heaven and earth and sea,
and everything that is in them,
such he has as his abode.
He inspires all things,
he gives life to all things,
he stands above all things,
and he stands beneath all things.
He enlightens the light of the sun,
he strengthens the light of the night and the stars,
he makes wells in the arid land and dry islands in the sea,
and he places the stars in the service of the greater lights.
He has a Son who is co-eternal with himself,
and similar in all respects to himself;
and neither is the Son younger than the Father,
nor is the Father older than the Son;
and the Holy Spirit breathes in them.
And the Father and the Son and Holy Spirit are inseparable.
[Amen.]

Litany of the Trinity[5]

(*May be sung Litany style*)

have mercy upon us, O God the Father Almíghty,
   O *God* of Hosts,
   O Hígh God,
O Lord of *all* the world,
O inéffable God,
O Creator *of* the Elements.

Have mercy upon us, O Almighty God,
Jesus Christ, Son of the Living Gód,
O *Son* twice-born,
O Only-begotten of God the Fáther,
O First born of the *Vir*gin Mary,
O beginning of áll things,
O completion *of* the world,
O Wórd of God,
O Way to the heav*en*ly Kingdom,
O life of áll things,
O Intelligence of the *my*stic world.

Have mercy upon us, O God Almíghty,
O *Holy* Spirit;
O Spirit that is highest of all spírits,
O Fing*er* of God,
O Protection of all Chrístians,
O Comforter *of* the sorrowful,
O Clément one,
O merciful *Inter*cessor,
O Imparter of true wiśdom,
O Author of the *Holy* Scriptures,
O Ruler of spéech,
O Sp*ir*it of wisdom,

O Spirit of understánding,
O Sp*ir*it of counsel,
O Spirit of stréngth,
O Sp*ir*it of knowledge,
O Spirit from whom is ordered every lofty thińg.
O Holy Spirit you rule all created things,
visible *and* invisible,
Have mer*cy* upon us.

O Almighty God, the heavenly Fáther,
and the only-beg*ott*en Son,
Have mercy upón us.
Have mer*cy* upon us,
O Father, O Son, O Holy Spírit.
Have mercy upon us, O *only* God,
O God of heaven, have mercy upon us.
Have mercy upon *us*, O God
from whom and through whom
is the rule of all created things for you, O God,
To whom be glory and honour
for ever and ever.
Amen.

Absolution

May almighty God have mercy on us,
forgive us our sins,
and bring us to everlasting life.
Amen.

Holy Sprinkling (*optional*)

THE PEACE

Celebrant: Lord Jesus Christ, you said to your apostles 'I leave you peace, my peace I give you.' Look not on our sins, but on the faith of your Church, and grant us the peace and unity of your Kingdom where you live for ever and ever. Amen.

The Peace of the Lord be with you always;
and with your spirit.

THE OFFERTORY

Celebrant: Thank you, O Lord God Almighty,
Thank you for the earth and the waters,
Thank you for the sky, the air and the sun,
Thank you for all living creatures.

Come, O Lord, in the Bread of Life.

Celebrant: Praise be to you, O Lord God Almighty,
For our homes, our families,
Our friends, and loved ones.
Praise be to you for all the people
Around us everywhere in this wounded world.

Come, O Lord, in the Cup of Healing.

The Prayer over the Gifts

The Great Thanksgiving

The Lord be with you,
and with your spirit.
Let us give thanks to the Lord our God.
It is right to give our thanks and praise.

The Stowe Preface[6]

Father, all powerful and ever-living God,
   we do well always and everywhere to give you thanks
   through Jesus Christ our Lord.
You [O Father], with your only-begotten Son and the Holy Spirit are
   God.
You are God, one immortal;
You are God, incorruptible and unmoving;
You are God, invisible and faithful;
You are God, wonderful and worthy of praise;
You are God, strong and worthy of honour;
You are God, most high and magnificent;
You are God, living and true;
You are God, wise and powerful;
You are God, holy and splendid;
You are God, great and good;
You are God, awesome and peace-loving;
You are God, beautiful and righteous;
You are God, pure and kind;
You are God, blessed and just;
You are God, tender and holy;
You are God, not in the singularity of one person,
   but in the Trinity of substance.

We believe you;
We bless you;
We adore you;
and praise your name for evermore.
We praise you
through Christ who is the salvation of the universe;
through Christ who is the life of human beings;
through Christ who is the resurrection of the dead.

Through him the angels praise your majesty;
the dominations adore;
the powers of the heaven of heavens tremble;
the virtues and the blessed seraphim
concelebrate in exultation;
so grant, we pray you,
that our voices may be admitted to that of the chorus,
in humble declaration of your glory,
as we say/sing:

Holy, holy, holy Lord
God of power and might,
heaven and earth are full of your glory.
Hosanna in the highest.

Blessed is he who comes in the name of the Lord.
Hosanna in the highest.

Eucharistic Prayer[7]

Most merciful Father, we humbly pray and implore you, through Jesus Christ your Son, our Lord, to be pleased to receive and bless these gifts, these holy unblemished offerings.

We offer them to you in the first place for your holy Church throughout the whole world. Be pleased to keep her in peace, to watch over her, and to gather her in unity and to guide her and also for *N.* your servant our bishop and all the bishops and all right believing teachers of the Catholic apostolic faith.

Remember, Lord, your servants and handmaids *N.* and *N.* and all here present whose faith and devotion are known to you. We offer for them, or they themselves offer, this sacrifice of praise for themselves and all their own, for the redeeming of their souls, for their hope of safety and salvation; and they now send up their prayers to you, the eternal, living and true God.

Being in fellowship we reverently bring to mind, firstly the glorious Mary, ever virgin, Mother of our God and Lord Jesus Christ, and then your blessed apostles and martyrs; Peter and Paul, Andrew, James, Bartholomew, Matthew, Simon and Jude, David, Ninian and Patrick, Columba, Teilo, Brigid, Deiniol and Samson, Asaph, Illtud, Dyfrig, Petroc, Padarn and all your saints: grant by their merits and prayers that at all times we may be defended and helped by your protection. Through the same Christ our Lord.

   Amen.

Be pleased, O God, to bless this offering, to accept it fully, to make it perfect and worthy to please you, so that it may become for us the Body and Blood of your dearly beloved Son, our Lord Jesus Christ.

Who the day before he suffered took bread into his holy and venerable hands, and with his eyes lifted up to heaven, to you, God, his almighty Father, giving thanks to you, he blessed, broke and gave it to his disciples saying: Take and eat you all of this, for this is my body.

In like manner, after he had supped, taking also this chalice into his holy and venerable hands again giving thanks to you, he blessed and gave it to his disciples, saying: Take and drink you all of this for this is the chalice of my blood, of the new and eternal testament: the mystery of faith: which shall be shed for you and for many for the remission of sins. As often as you shall do these things, you shall do them in memory of me.

Wherefore, Lord, in memory of the blessed passion of the same Christ, your Son, our Lord, of his resurrection from among the dead and of his ascension to heavenly glory, we your servants and with all your holy people offer to your sovereign majesty, from among your gifts bestowed upon us, a victim perfect, holy and spotless, the holy bread of everlasting life and the chalice of everlasting salvation.

Be pleased to look upon these offerings with a favourable and gracious countenance; accept them as you were pleased to accept the offerings of your servant Abel the righteous, the sacrifice of our father Abraham, and that of Melchisedech, your high priest, a holy sacrifice, a spotless victim.

We humbly implore you, almighty God, be these offerings to be carried by the hands of your holy angel to your altar on high, in the sight of your divine majesty, that all who are partakers at the altar of the precious Body and Blood of your Son, may be filled with all heavenly grace and blessing. Through the same Christ our Lord.

 Amen.

Remember, also, Lord, your servants and handmaids N. and N. who are gone hence before us, marked with the sign of faith, and sleep the sleep of peace. To them, Lord, and to all that rest in Christ, grant, we implore you, a place of happiness, light and peace. Through the same Christ our Lord.

 Amen.

To us, also, your sinful servants, who hope in the multitude of your mercies, be pleased to grant some place and fellowship with your holy apostles and martyrs and all your saints. We pray you admit us into their company, not weighing our own merits but bestowing on us your own free pardon. Through Christ our Lord.

Through him, O Lord, you ever create these good things, and you hallow, quicken and bless them as gifts for us.

By him and with him and in him are ever given to you, God the Father Almighty, in the unity of the Holy Spirit all honour and glory for ever and ever.

Amen.

The Holy Communion

As our Saviour taught us, we boldly pray:

Our Father who art in heaven,
hallowed be thy name,
thy Kingdom come,
thy will be done,
on earth as it is in heaven.
Give us this day our daily bread.
And forgive us our trespasses,
as we forgive those who trespass against us.
And lead us not into temptation
but deliver us from evil.
For thine is the Kingdom,
the power, and the glory,
for ever and ever.
Amen.

Deliver us, we implore you, Lord, from all evils, past, present and to come, and by the intercession of the blessed and glorious Mary ever virgin, Mother of God, and of your blessed apostles Peter and Paul, and of Andrew and all the saints, mercifully give peace in our days; that through the help of your mercy we may always be free from sin and safe from all troubles. Through the same Jesus Christ, your Son, our Lord, who lives and reigns with you in the unity of the Holy Spirit, one God, for ever and ever.

Amen.

The Fraction of the Host

(From the *Stowe Missal*[8])

They recognized the Lord, Alleluia;
In the breaking of the loaf, Alleluia [Lk 24:35];
For the loaf that we break is the body
of our Lord Jesus Christ, Alleluia;
The cup which we bless is the blood
of our Lord Jesus Christ, Alleluia [1 Cor 10:16–17];
For the remission of our sins, Alleluia [Mt 26:28];
O Lord, let your mercy come upon us, Alleluia;
In you O Lord have I put my trust, Alleluia [Ps 31:1];
They recognized the Lord, Alleluia;
In the breaking of the loaf, Alleluia [Lk 24:35].

Celebrant: O Lord, we believe that in this breaking of your body and pouring out of your blood we become your redeemed people;
We confess that in taking the gifts of this pledge here, we lay hold in hope of enjoying its true fruits in the heavenly places.

Agnus Dei

Jesus, Lamb of God:
have mercy on us.
Jesus, bearer of our sins:
have mercy on us.
Jesus, redeemer of the world:
give us your peace.

or   Lamb of God, you take away the sins of the world: have mercy on us.

**Lamb of God, you take away the sins of the world:
have mercy on us.
Lamb of God, you take away the sins of the world:
grant us peace.**

Celebrant: Jesus is the Lamb of God who takes away the sins of the world. Happy are those who are called to his supper.
**Lord, I am not worthy to receive you,
but only say the word and I shall be healed.**

The Communion Antiphon

The Celebrant receives Holy Communion and says:

He gives heavenly bread to the hungry,
And to the thirsty water from the living spring.

Christ the Lord himself comes, who is Alpha and Omega.
He shall come again to judge us all.

Come, you holy ones, receive the body of Christ,
Drinking the holy blood by which you were redeemed.

The Sacrament is administered with these words:

The Body of Christ.
Amen.
The Blood of Christ.
Amen.

A Hymn may be sung during Communion.

Prayer after Communion
(see Appendix)

The Dismissal

The Lord be with you;
And with your spirit.

The Priest may say this or a different blessing:

The peace of God which passes all understanding, keep your hearts and minds in the knowledge and love of God, and of his Son, Jesus Christ our Lord: and the blessing of God Almighty, the Father, the Son and the Holy Spirit, be amongst you and remain with you always.
Amen.

Let us go forth in peace;
In the name of Christ.
Amen.

or

I bless you, in the name of the Father, the Son, and the Sacred Spirit, the One and the Three. May God give you to drink of his cup, the sun shine bright upon you, may the night call down peace and when you come into his household may the door be open wide for you to go in to your joy.

Go in peace to love and serve the Lord.
In the name of Christ.
Amen.

Recessional Hymn

MAY THE ROAD RISE
    TO MEET YOU,
MAY THE WIND BE
    ALWAYS AT YOUR BACK,
MAY THE SUN SHINE
    WARM UPON YOUR FACE,
MAY THE RAINS FALL
    SOFT UPON YOUR FIELDS.
UNTIL WE MEET AGAIN,
MAY GOD HOLD YOU IN
    THE HOLLOW OF HIS HAND.

From the Gaelic
(taken from Celtic Blessings *by Brendan O'Malley)*

NOTES

1. Adapted by the author.
2. Antiphonary of Bangor VIII Century, 'The Lighting of the Vesper Light or Paschal Candle'; translated by Dr Oliver Davies.
3. The Gloria is the modern translation, International Committee on English in the Liturgy, Inc (ICEL) 1983.
4. Tírechán's Creed from *The Patrician Texts from the Book of Armagh* AD670 (Dublin) Ludwig Bieler; translated by Dr Thomas O'Loughlin.
5. The Litany of the Trinity – adapted from the Litany of the same title by Mugron, the coarb of Columba in Ireland and Scotland, i.e., Abbot of the Federated Columban Monasteries in the two countries of which the chief were respectively Iona in Scotland and Durrow in Ireland. Mugron held the abbacy from 964 to 980 (Plummer, *Irish Litanies*, 1925).
6. The Stowe Preface – a translation of the preface from the *Stowe Missal* by Dr Thomas O'Loughlin; adapted by Brendan O'Malley. The *Stowe Missal* was owned by the Marquis of Buckinghamshire, of Stowe House. It is the oldest book from the early Irish Church still extant. It is of monastic origin linked with Tallaght and dated to the eighth/early ninth centuries. It is now in the Royal Irish Academy in Dublin.
7. *Stowe Missal* Eucharistic Prayer – an adapted translation of the canon of St Gelasius (AD494) which was not further revised until AD600. (In the *Stowe Missal* it is labelled, 'the Canon of the lord Pope Gelasius'.) I have removed the reference to 'N. our Pope' and added local Celtic saints alongside the universal college of bishops. I have done this as an ecumenical gesture without in any way denying the Petrine Primacy.
8. 'Congruerunt Dominum'; translated by Dr Thomas O'Loughlin.

APPENDIX: ALTERNATIVE PRAYERS AND SENTENCES

Additional Prayers I

Sentence

You are my strength Lord, I will love you,
Under the shadow of your wings protect me.

The Prayers of Mugron

Opening Prayer

Kindle in our hearts, O God,
The flame of love that never ceases,
That it may burn in us, giving light to others.
May we shine for ever in your temple,
Set on fire with your eternal light,
Even your Son, Jesus Christ,
Our Saviour and Redeemer.
Amen.

St Columba

Prayer over the Gifts

Lord God,
May the gifts we offer increase our love for you
And bring us to eternal life.

Communion Sentence

He gives heavenly bread to the hungry,
And to the thirsty, water from the living spring.

Prayer after Communion

We believe, O Lord, that in this breaking of your body and pouring out of your blood we become redeemed people. We confess that by our sharing of this sacrament we are strengthened to endure in hope until we lay hold and enjoy its true fruits in the heavenly places.

Stowe Missal

Additional Prayers II

Sentence

Let us adore the Lord,
Maker of marvellous works,
Bright heaven with its angels,
And on earth the white-waved sea.

Ancient Irish

Opening Prayer

O Lord Jesus Christ, you are the way, the truth and the life: suffer us not to stray from you, who are the way, nor to distrust you, who are the truth, nor to rest in any other thing than you, who are the life. Teach us by your Holy Spirit what to believe, what to do, and wherein to take our rest. We ask it for your Name's sake. Amen.

Erasmus

Prayer over the Gifts

Praise to you, O Christ,
King of eternal glory!
Man does not live on bread alone,
But on every word that comes from the mouth of God.
Praise to you, O Christ,
King of eternal glory!

Communion Sentence

This is the living bread which comes down from heaven,
He who eats of it shall live for ever.

Prayer after Communion

Lord, may we be wakeful at sunrise to begin a new day for you;
Cheerful at sunset for having done our work for you;
Thankful at moonrise and under starshine for the beauty of your
 universe;
And may we add what little may be in us to add to your great world.
Amen.

The Abbot of Greve

Additional Prayers III

Sentence

The King is knocking.
If you would have your share of heaven on earth,
Open the door of your heart
And let in the King.

Hebridean

Opening Prayer

O God, your name is blessed from the rising of the sun to its setting; fill our hearts with knowledge of yourself and our mouths with your praise, that from East to West all may sing your glory, with one voice and with one accord, in Jesus Christ, your Son, our Lord. Amen.

Prayer over the Gifts

God our Creator,
May this bread and wine we offer
As a sign of love and worship
Lead us to eternal joy.

Communion Sentence

We know and believe in God's love for us.

Prayer after Communion

See that you are at peace among yourselves, my children,
And love one another in Jesus, the Christ, our Lord.

St Columba